The Teachings of The Band

Channeled Wisdom for Personal Growth

Willow Sibert

Peak Aspirations Press

Copyright © 2024 by Willow Sibert and Peak Aspirations LLC, DBA Peak Aspirations Press

All rights reserved.

No portion of this book may be reproduced in any form without written permission from the publisher or author, except as permitted by U.S. copyright law.

Contents

PREFACE	1
Acknowledgements	9
1. An Introduction to The Band	11
2. Asking the Questions	15
3. What's it like to Channel The Band?	19
4. Soul, Spirit, and Personality	23
5. The Plan	41
6. Living in the Moment	43
7. Time	45
8. Healing in Time, Healing in Lifetimes	49

9.	Incarnation: Look to Nature For the Answers	61
10.	Beings from Other Planets: We and They	67
11.	The Path of the Soul	71
12.	Living the Life That is Guided	73
13.	Abundance	91
14.	Physical and Non-Physical Energy	95
15.	The World at Large	99
16.	Male vs. Female Energy	123
17.	Being in the Flow	127
18.	Standing for Who You Are	135
19.	A Beginning	138
About the Author		143
Claim Your Free Gift		145
Review This Book		146

PREFACE

As a child, I remember watching my mother sit at the kitchen table and have a conversation with Grandma. She'd asked questions and Grandma would answer. She talked to lots of people at that table – old friends, relatives, Native Americans – people she knew and people she'd never met. When she spoke with them, she'd ask a question aloud and then grab a pen or pencil, hold it over a tablet of paper, and wait for the answer.

You see, the people she talked to weren't really there. These were people who were dead – no longer in a body – spirits (or ghosts!) – and when she talked to them, they communicated by automatic writing.

Every time any of my aunts and uncles came to visit, the adults would gather in the kitchen and talk to these people, too. The entire family, on both my Mom and Dad's sides, liked to chat with "whoever would come in." By the time I was eight years old, I, too, was sitting at that table talking and writing. I figured if my Mom could "talk" to these people, so could I!

I come from a long line of psychics – mostly on the female side of Mom's family. My Mom did automatic writing, her mom did it, and so did her mom. Mom used to tell me stories of my great aunt and her sister "working the table," trying to get spirits to talk to them by moving a small wooden table. The table was the precursor to the Ouija™ Board.

As a child, my dad's family attended a Spiritualist church. His mother was a hands-on healer and his dad, a medical intuitive. They participated in trumpet séances and my grandfather even had his own trumpet. I always say that my psychic gifts are genetic – it's in my genes, from both my parents and their families.

When I was a teenager, we found people who could go into a trance. Our Saturday nights would be spent sitting in the living room, drinking sodas and coffee, waiting for someone to "come in" and talk to us while in this trance. I had become pretty good at getting messages through automatic writing, but the messages were always in my head before I began writing. One day I asked my Mom if I could just say the words instead of writing them, and she said, "Yes." That simple change became life-altering and allowed me to speak the words that came to me from spirit instead of putting them to paper.

I spent my early adulthood learning all I could about psychic phenomena. I took crystal healing courses, psychic development classes, and worked with a mentor for many years. I knew I could "do" things and "get" information, but I didn't know what to do with this gift.

I eventually found my way to a corporate career, spending 14 years at a computer company where I held evening meditation sessions, gave readings, and used my natural healing abilities to relieve co-workers of headaches and other pains. And even though I was developing a successful career, every year I would ask my guidance, "Can I go now?" I couldn't figure out why I was working in this environment of suits, business plans, and budgets. And every time I'd get the same answer, "No. You're not done."

***

One day while on a business trip to Dallas, Texas, I saw something on an early morning show that caught my eye. It was a show about a woman-owned ranch and it spoke to my sense of nature and freedom. Once again, as I had done year after year, I asked my guidance, "Can I go now?"

I didn't hear the usual "No." In fact I heard nothing but silence. I asked the question again, and this time I got a feeling, first in the pit of my stomach and then in my chest that something was about to change. After the third, "Can I go now?" I knew it was time to go. I'd finally gotten the "yes" I'd been asking for. On the plane back to California, I told my boyfriend I was leaving the company. He looked at me and said, "You are crazy!"

Ten weeks later, crazy or not, I was gone. I left my job, my retirement, 401K, stock options, and financial security. I put everything I owned in storage, bought a 20-foot travel traveler, and headed out for parts unknown with my dog, Jackson. I traveled up and down the west coast, then through Utah, Nevada, Colorado, and finally landed in Tucson, Arizona.

I began searching for the 'real work' I was to do, using all the tools I'd been born with and those I'd learned along the way as a result of this quest. I became a certified hypnotherapist, a coach, and with a leap of faith, I admitted openly to being a psychic and channel. I found my new work profoundly rewarding and more and more I began doing psychic readings for people. My work felt so natural that I even got the courage to put it on a business card.

In the spring of 1998, my meditations began to change. Instead of the usually quiet space I would go to, I felt as if there was an entity nearby. This entity was asking if it could use my body to move around. Not keen on having anyone or anything messing with my body, I said, "No." After a few weeks of this entity's constant nagging, I gave in and said, "OK. You can move my arms and head – but nothing else." Together, this entity and I would move my head and lift both my arms as we got a sense of each other. It reminded me of my two dogs when they first met. Circling each other, sniffing, retreating, not quite sure what to make of each other, until finally their comfort levels increased, and they would lay next to each other – as if they had known each other their entire lives.

That was the way it was with this presence and me. We circled, we sniffed, we retreated, and we looked each other in the eyes (well, sort of, as they were actually looking in through my eyes) until we felt comfortable with each other. All during this introduction period, I kept a journal. In my journaling, this entity found an easy way to communicate with me. I asked them who they were. They said their name was *"The Band."* They told me about themselves, some of the personalities within this band of energy, and what they were here for.

They also took me in my meditation to what looked like an executive boardroom, complete with an oval table with many chairs around it. Sitting there in those chairs were some faces I recognized: Albert Einstein, Ben Franklin, and Thomas Jefferson. It's this boardroom that I see now every time I channel. *The Band* and I sit around the very same table, and there's always a discussion going on between the members. Sometimes they even let *me* have a say!

My channeling has continued since then, becoming more and more a part of who I am and the work I do. People from all over the United States have come to hear the words of *The Band,* and the messages they give. They are an inspiration, a guiding light, and for me, a profound gift. Every day I am grateful for *The Band* and their sense of humor, their enlightened thinking, and their connection to Divine Knowledge. It is this profound gift that I share with all who read this book.

FAST FORWARD... 2024. It's hard to believe that the original material for this book was channeled beginning in 2002 and it's now finally being shared with everyone who is intrigued by the question "what else is there?" As for me, I've gone through a myriad of changes since 2002, but the one thing that has always remained constant was my connection to '*The Band*.' We are forever... like a circle that has no beginning and no ending... The messages we share at this time are also like a circle... no beginning and no ending. They are what they are. TIMELESS.

Thank you for being part of the Circle. W

In Light,

Willow Sibert

Acknowledgements

Thank you to the 'Broad Band'

This book is a labor of love that began with the dedication of 12 women who heard *The Band* speak and wanted to be part of the message. They opened their homes and their hearts for eight weeks while we met to hear that message.

Their questions and focus allowed *The Band* and me to simply speak the message without any thought to the hows or whys.

These women even named themselves "The Broad Band" – a play on words – first because they were all "broads," and second because of their love for *The*

Band. I will be forever grateful to all of them for the love and support they gave me to make this book happen.

Since then, there have been many more groups of people, gathering, listening, and sharing the messages from *The Band*. To everyone who has participated in a channeling with *The Band*, thank you. We will be eternally grateful for the love and support you have given us.

And lastly, I'd like to thank Iris Bell, whose loving support has made this all happen. She has been a guiding light, believing in this work and me when I had my doubts. Her skills at editing and her perseverance in insisting on this being published have been unwavering. Thank you, Iris, for your friendship, your kindness, and your love.

An Introduction to The Band

Good Evening...

We are *The Band*. We are a collection of energy. We are a frequency of knowledge. We are a band of energy in which contain the personalities and memories of many whom you have known from the past or are learning about in the present. We join together in this frequency to bring you information, share knowledge, and assist in bringing the consciousness of the planet forward. No one person can raise his or her level of awareness – can rise up in the spiritual quest, unless ALL do.

Just as a band is a collection of musical instruments that when played well and played together form one sound, one harmony, one note if you will, we, too, are a band who speak as one voice. There may be times when we speak as individual voices just as there may be a musical solo in a concert. We are a band, a circle -- no beginning, no end. But it is complete. It is ongoing. And that is who we are.

Within *The Band* are contained the personalities and knowledges of Albert Einstein, Benjamin Franklin, Thomas Jefferson, Samuel Hahnemann, and Marie Curie. We have an infinite number of souls whose frequency may be in part and parcel integrated with us. Pierre Teilhard de Chardin, Amelia Earhart, and Isaac Newton are also members of our Band.

We Are Not Separate

So we are truly unique and yet we are truly a part of you. Nothing is separate in this Universe. There is not one person that is separate from the other and you are not separate from the trees or the birds or the animals or any of the plants. You are all part of One. It is that One that has brought you here together at this time. For there is much going on in this planet, in this Universe. There is much going on in this whole Oneness that is causing people to come together. For there is a collective consciousness about you as well as there is a collective consciousness about us.

And together we are part of the One and together we have a mission; work to do. But it truly is not work when it is your passion. When it is your path. It simply is. It is what you are here for. It is what we are here for because we are all together.

Asking the Questions

We know that there are many questions in this room today for we hear them without the voices - but what is very important for each and every one of you is the asking of the question. When you ask the question, it means you are ready for the answer. So even though there are those in the nonphysical who can provide you with all the answers to all the questions, it is because of choice, of free will, and your growth that it is necessary for you to ask the question. True knowledge comes from the questions, not from the answer.

You see, one of the things that is extremely important for us and extremely important for you to realize is that the answer is not the most important thing, for it is in the question where your answer lies. When you ask a question, it is because you are ready to hear the answer. So we may push and we may prod you to ask a question. Answers and information are there for everyone and it is only in the moment when you are ready for that information, it appears. You never ask for anything more than you can handle. And you are never given anything more than that as well.

So, as you look at your lives and you go forth in your day, you wonder sometimes how much more can I take? How much more can I handle? Be assured, you never get anymore than you can handle. You need to remember also, that you have many guides and many angels and many spirits present with you at all times. You are never alone. And yet one of the guiding principles that we all live by is that we are there to help, but we do not interfere. Unless you ask.

So, as you go about your days in the coming weeks, do not forget to ask for help. Not only do you want to ask for help from those in the physical presence, but please pay special attention to us in the nonphysical. Because we are truly the other part of you. We are not separate. We exist with you and around you and we are simply in the nonphysical right now as you are in the physical. Does this make sense to you?

What you will find is that there are many, many people tapping into the knowledge. There are books that have been written, books that will be written, and books that are currently being written. There are channels and there are people who have tapped into the knowledge, so though some of the words may change a bit, the idea or the information is the same. That is what you all need to keep in mind. It is not the name that is important.

It is no accident that those of you who are here today have been brought here and it is no accident that those that are not here are not here. For always it is a gathering that is perfect. And those who are in our presence are creating that perfection. For the physicals and non-physicals that are here in this room at this time are to perpetuate the information, to allow it to come forth in a way that is necessary and needed.

And so, we wish to say to you, be sure that you know that when you show up for the meetings, you are guided to be here. And when you do not, do not even give it a second thought. Everything is moving forward in a perfect and timely manner, even though the lack of time is something that gives us time. That is another profundity. Each and every week we shall try and come up with one of those. At least one.

What's it like to Channel The Band?

A Conversation with Willow Sibert

The frequency of *The Band* is the same thing as a soul grouping; only they refer to it as frequencies. That's why there are different bands of knowledge. For them to be in that frequency there's no separation or differentiation. It's all one voice. If someone would say, "Yo, Al, can you come in and talk?" then all his little particles would come together and my hair would get frizzy. I would feel all these little particles collecting together.

It's fascinating to sense that within this Band there's this diversity among The Band participants.

It's like I'm sitting at a conference table. The table is so real at times that I don't feel like I can move my body forward or I will hit the table with my chest. I can't actually see *The Band*, but there are all these people around. A question comes in and it feels like we have a five-minute conversation. *The Band* members are discussing the answer, and sometimes I'm saying, "You can't say that," or "I don't want to say that," and I'm told to quit arguing and just say the words.

I guess that's because I don't go into a deep trance state and so I'm aware of what's going on physically in the room. I get to participate in the discussion, but I'm not allowed to change the answer! When the answer is spoken it's only been a second or so since the question was asked even though it felt like five minutes. I seem to go into some sort of time warp and time is expanded.

Do you get visuals?

I don't actually see the picture. I get the knowing. When they're talking, and they give an answer, I get a sense of dimension that goes very deep. It's as if the answer that is given may be dimensionally 5 inches deep, but the knowledge behind it is 3 feet deep, if that makes sense. There's so much more to the answer than is spoken because the words aren't there or we're not ready or the concept hasn't been defined yet. Typically for the three days after a channeling session, I continue to get all this information. It has to filter through.

I know at the very beginning you mentioned some of the personalities. I'm curious about what the common thing that makes it a unified group?

They tell me that they come together as a band of thinkers whose metaphysical knowledge is of a common frequency.

Are there other Bands?

Absolutely. That's what they showed me when I went to Walden Pond in Concord, MA. Also, one of the Broad Band members did some channeling herself and came up with twenty names of people she says are in *The Band*. I believe she's right.

I'm wondering if Nicholas Tesla is there.

I think so. What they realized was that even though they tapped into the scientific part of knowledge when they were alive, what they were talking about was very limited in terms of reality. Half of what they were talking about was not real.

I asked as a joke if they were disappointed we weren't asking scientific questions.

What they really are thinkers. The one thing I remember *The Band* telling me is that numbers are the highest order of things. Because you go from the most complex to the simplest, the simplest being the highest order. They showed me the whole thing. At the base chakra, the lowest level is words. Words become literature and music becomes something else and up at the top is numbers.

Soul, Spirit, and Personality

Stewards of the Planet

What we wish to say about stewardship is that each and every one of you is a steward or stewardess in your own right. You are caretakers, you are guardians, you are messengers. Each and every one of you in your own unique and blessed way is about turning on the light for others.

Why are we here?

You each have your own specific mission. You each have your own specific calling. No two people travel the same path. However, there are times such as this that your paths are so close together it feels like one, and you come together as the One. It is times like this we will be sharing. After the sharing has been completed, you will be taking your message, your knowledge to others. As we have said in the past, the ripple effect continues. So with each word, with each piece of knowledge, with each person in this room, we are causing change to occur. Nothing will ever remain the same. And that is a good thing.

What is the soul? What is the spirit, and how do they relate?

When we speak of soul, what we are referring to within an individual soul is that which encompasses all of the lifetimes, all of the knowledges, all of the essences of an individual being. That is a soul. So each one of you is part and parcel of a soul. You have within your soul-being all that you ever were and all you ever will be. Your soul, in essence, is expanding. If you were to actually picture it, your body would be here, and your soul (if you were to give it a boundary) would be very, very, large around you. Your soul could really be your higher self.

What we refer to as your spirit is the soul that is incarnated. Your spirit is that part of the soul that is in the body. The spirit changes and is part of the soul. One is part of the other. The spirit has a time element to it. It is a specific embodiment of soul.

How does that all relate to personality?

When you are a soul and your spirit has incarnated into this body, then the human form that is created or that which is impacted by the environment, relationships, your family, is what we refer to as your personality. The spirit then is that piece of the soul that is attached to personality traits. This person has knowledge about this and is very outgoing. How you define that person is how we define personality. Do not confuse it with the personality, as psychologists would use it.

Psychologists are always trying to put a personality into a box. They are always trying to define it as this type of personality or that type of personality. We use personality in a bigger frame. For instance, when we say the personality of Albert Einstein is with us, we mean what Albert Einstein did in his life and his knowledges. The whole of that person in that specific life is what we refer to as that personality. Albert Einstein is only part of that large soul. He is only one part of who he is or who he has been.

When the soul decides to incarnate into another body; it chooses, for instance, things it wants to experience or experience again in a different way. In some way we could say that the personality from the previous life could influence the incarnation of the next iteration if you will. It would influence the new personality it comes in so it would be remembering.

All that exists within the soul is there all the time and available to tap into. When a person is incarnated into a weaker body or a weaker frame of mind there is a leakage or bleed-through. Then other personalities come through and there are leakages from times before. That would be a messy thing, and there have been many.

Is that ever defined as multiple personalities?

It is quite possible, and that is one definition of that, yes. There is that possibility that other personalities leak through and so there is a multipleness to them. However, that is not the only case of that. Sometimes a traumatic experience causes the division of the personality into age groups.

Going from spirit to soul and then up another level, we're all connected into one source. How does all that work?

Ah, very good. It is as if you have one cell that is individual but that one cell is part of something larger. Each individual soul is actually part of the larger one soul. There are many thoughts along these ideas. There are groupings of souls. What we would say to you is not to get so locked into the idea of having to define everything. Because you see as you are expanding and learning, the first thing that happens is you want a definition for everything. You want order. The more you have order, the more you realize there is no order and there is total order.

We could spend weeks and weeks and weeks going into all the groupings of the soul. But let us say that you are part of a group soul that is part of another group and eventually you all connect with the one soul, that beginning source of energy that contains all of us, all that ever has been, all that ever will be. It is no accident that cells divide and multiply. You have so much to learn from how your own body replicates, how a cell replicates, how a soul replicates. There is no accident. That way of being had to come from somewhere. It didn't just get made up.

Why are we bothering to be separate souls?

Are you asking, "What's the purpose of being separate if all we're trying to do is reconnect?" Well, there is that old saying, "Curiosity killed the cat." And "Satisfaction brought him back." If you want to get real simple about it, it was the curiosity, the need to explore, the need to see the potential of what the soul could do. There became a feeling, a wanting to explore, a wanting to know things in a different way. So truly being connected, the soul decided to incarnate here into an earth body, to experience different things they could not experience any other place, to have that ability to choose, to express, and feel emotion.

Those are the two things that make this earth plane unique: choice and emotion. Particularly emotion. When you think of all the emotions possible, all the positive emotions, the joy, compassion, love, understanding, sense of good will, and camaraderie.

For every positive emotion, there's a negative one; there's a mirror. When there was a perfect utopia of being able to experience all the emotions, everyone remained connected even though they were individual. Remember there is choice and people could choose to feel anger and hate and greed and larceny and everything on the other side of the fence of the positive.

The more we experienced pain and the more humans experienced all of the different feelings a human is capable of — and mind you, most of you in the room have only experienced a tenth of the emotions that could be experienced — the more the forgetting started. The more that one is greedy, the more one thinks of himself or herself only.

That is when the sense of separation came. The heavy emotions, the anger, the rage... caused separation. They caused people to pull back from others, caused souls to be disconnected. So what is occurring now is that groups like this here and groups all over the world are coming together again to remember and be reconnected in the positive sense and shifting the energy and shifting the emotions as well. We are recreating the oneness.

We were never meant to be separate. Having the choice of what emotions to experience could in itself lead to separation, and it did.

One of the emotions you didn't mention is fear. Is that the overlying negative energy? It seems to me all the ones you did mention all come from fear.

Yes. If we were to say what is on the other side of love, it is fear. A lack of knowing. It is easier to shift someone who is ignorant than to shift someone who has the knowledge and has decided they do not want to live in the positive. In ignorance, it is as if there hasn't been a choice made yet. It simply is. They are just there in a state of limbo. It is neither a knowing nor a choosing.

Is there anything to be learned by fear?

We think there is something to be learned by all things, so yes. What is to be learned from fear is how forceful and powerful fear is. Think about those people who have truly ascended, those who have faced even the greatest of physical threats to their lives and their bodies and are not living in fear. They live in total peace and harmony with what is. They allow whatever is to move through them. There is always a choice. Many people don't realize what they've got until fear comes into their life. It's like holding up a mirror to show them who they are and what they really have and what they are really experiencing.

As the emotions began to grow and be experienced, they spread out from the core of joy, happiness, compassion, and love, and moved out to the fringes, to the negative sides of these emotions. Those living in fear or anger then became guided by someone of a like-resonance. Like attracted like. The voice they heard in their ears was not for the highest and best good but the less than positive. We really do stay away from the word "evil." We do not accept that word.

I'd like to ask a question about the negative versus positive. We've talked about that and the need to be more positive, and yet the negative, so to speak, has some kind of goal. It exists. This is how the world operates: these polarities. Can you comment on the negative from the bigger point of view where it's accepted?

We are very glad you asked for that clarification. Because clarity is what we're here for. In a balanced world, you have equal amounts. Yes, there is a place for the negative. You can call them plusses and minuses if you will. The on and off switch.

When that balance is even, then life is even and it is in its perfect harmony. What has happened throughout the ages in the world is we have become out of balance. We are not saying to get rid of the negative. What we are truly saying is to return to a state of balance, of perfect harmony. Excess negative must be turned into a positive to allow for the scales to even out.

But are you saying all negative has to be turned into positive?

It is not about getting rid of negative. It is about having the world in perfect harmony.

For instance, when you create mulch, it is because you put things together in a pile and you allow them to rot, so to speak. You are creating this turbulence, this icky goo no one wants to be around. However, when you take that and put that into the soil, it causes new things to grow. There is a purpose and a plan and it needs to be an ebb and a flow. However, when it's at an ebb and it tugs and tugs and tugs, something's going to snap.

Would you agree that in the opposite way, if it's too positive that's also an imbalance?

It's a fine line. When there is almost too much positive, it doesn't flow right. It doesn't move. However when we truly get back to the one state, the one soul, the one source, that which we are incarnating over and over again and aspiring to be, then the purity of the soul, of the positive, becomes such that there is no need for an ebb and a flow. It is as if everything becomes pure light in almost a different state, a different dimension. That's when it shifts. For life to occur on the earth plane, there has to be a give and a take, an ebb and a flow. Those are words you learned since the time you were born.

Could you comment on the role of emotions in coloring our experience of that? It seems it is emotions that color the experience that we interpret as being a quote "bad" or "good" thing, versus just enjoying the life that occurs regardless of the form.

Okay, let me give an example. The actor Christopher Reeve had a very debilitating, horrendous accident. Now many people could have chosen to allow all of the negative states of emotions into their lives. "Life is totally destroyed, I've become an angry shriveled up being." Or they could see their lives as vital forces and use the positive energies or emotions to create lives that are still fulfilling and worthy, as he has. All life is worthy.

Do your thoughts control your emotions, or do your emotions control your thoughts? I think they can even be separate.

They are separate, but not inseparable.

When I find that I don't verbalize an emotion but just feel it, it's neither good nor bad, it's just so, it runs through me. But when I start making up a story or drama about it then it can be positive or negative.

For instance, anger could cause a young man to be so upset with his living situation, that he decides he is no longer going to live in that way. He does everything in his power to get out and he becomes very successful.

Then there is the anger that causes another person to be miserable. He can't function properly in this world because he can't get past his own anger. It is the use of that emotion, either toward a positive means, to moving a life forward, or allowing their life to be stuck where it is, or even ending their life.

Earlier, you were bringing up the idea that emotion is movement rather than being stuck.

Yes. Now getting into the very big picture, everything is perfect as it is. Even if this young man was so angry, he went off and killed people, he was still learning something. His soul will incarnate at another time to keep progressing through whatever he's going through. In that big sense, it's perfect. It's process. You could say that for everything that occurs. However, if you want to get down the microscope and take a look, it's all about the ability to take the sense of whom you are when you're in a meditative state and be that in your waking state.

If everything is perfect as it is, then I would surmise that beings that are ascending necessarily achieved a state of perfect balance or have they?

Yes, they have learned to move past that. They have learned to move beyond the emotions, to simply allow and be. It's as if the emotional experiences become smoke and they move through them instead of letting the experiences become attached to them.

Is there a difference in the present time in the preparedness of the people who are ascending or has it always been the same? Has the energy been hurried up?

Truly in ascension, there is no hurry. But are there frequencies vibrating at a faster rate as a whole planetary universal system does? Yes, but there is no hurry at least not in the way that humans define "hurry."

In a bigger sense can you address the balance of negative and positive energy here on earth and the movement of the positive?

If we're hearing you clearly, are you referring to what's going on in the world?

On the earth.

It truly is about ebb and flow so everything that is occurring in the earth that is pulling away will then return. It's always moving. Destruction and terrorism are out here now. Then it goes to peace and harmony and then it goes another way and it continues back and forth like this. It's all perfect. There's nothing wrong with the way the earth is moving back and forth.

However, when we get down to the microcosm level, the human level, we say, "What are the things we can do to shorten the ebb or the flow? Because we all know our thoughts are energy. We all know that we are all energy. All the thoughts that are put out there can be manifested, thoughts that say, "I am living in fear. I'm terrified that my life will end, that I'm going to hurt, that the world will blow up."

The energy that needs to be put out there instead is, "All is perfect as it is. Everything that happens is for the highest and best good. I am love. I am peace." If you want to be positive and negative, those are the thought patterns that need to be put out there to neutralize the terror thought patterns.

A thought pattern can be replaced with another thought pattern. "I can't find a parking space, or I never find a parking space" can be changed into "I can find a parking space" or "I can come home with $1,000 in my pocket."

How does God relate to all of this?

Ahhh, as much as possible.

I get the sense that this is all one fabulous experiment and when you turn human beings loose in a place where all things are possible through free will, the permutations are astonishing. He/She must be learning a lot.

It could never be a double blind experiment. We think that perhaps most everybody is blind to this experiment. But that is a good question about God. Is there one Universal Being? One Omnipotent Source? Whatever your beliefs, God is the one source. Whatever your name is, it's all the one source. We are all part of the one source, made of God, part of God, this one source from which we all came.

To our knowledge, and we've had some pretty good knowledges in our Band to think that there would be this one source sitting on this throne, looking through the clouds, saying, "What's going on down here with

Johnny? We'd better check it out," is not quite accurate. We think we'd better leave that to Sunday school.

It would be a synergistic system that creates more synergy as it builds or as it goes on.

Correct. Truly there is something to the chaos theory. It is closer to the theory of what is happening to us than most of us realize, that there really is a pattern to the chaos, and that the chaos is creating the pattern and the pattern is chaotic and it's all part of the unfolding. As each human being becomes more aware and tapped into his soul and knowing, then he gets a sense of that big picture, of an utter profound calm inside of himself that says, "This isn't all for naught. I am part of all of this. I am not alone. I am connected to every single being whether it be human, plant, or other."

That is why there is so much discussion about meditation or quiet time. It is the only time you quiet your mind, let go of your emotions, and hear the voice of the one, which is to hear the voice of every single other being. And it is a loud voice.

I want to comment on the image of the experiment. I really like the idea of us all being sent out without the remembering and knowing we're all going to find our way back home, it's really a nice image.

We chose to forget, but now most importantly we chose to remember and we're on our way home. We are past the ebbing and now we're flowing.

I also got the idea I don't need to worry about ascending, because it can happen in the blink of an eye or I can work at it every day.

We suggest you not work on it, just be it. It's not about work.

The Plan

The plan is that there be no plan, and that the plan creates itself. So if you think about that and that there is free will and choice and we come here with a lack of plan and we spend all our lives planning and then we spend the rest of our lives trying not to have so many plans. An interesting dilemma.

The plan will create itself. It's not "each human being will create a plan." The plan will manifest itself. In other words, your path, your life, your flow will create itself and it will continue to create itself. It's as if you're driving and you're going up a hill and it appears the road ends. That's as if "I have no plan. The road is stopping."

But you know that every time you get to the top of the hill, there's a road on the other side. That's a part of the trusting that we must have. Our path, the road we are traveling, continues forward even if we do not see it, even if you do not know the plan. So think about that. Know there always is a road when you get to the top of the hill, and if there is not, you can create one.

Living in the Moment

There is no other moment than NOW. And that is the true essence of time. Do you understand if you are truly in the moment, in the absolute now, there is no time? There is no necessity for time. It is all that has ever occurred and all that will ever occur. It is all right there in the moment. And then you are in this moment, and then in the next, and the next, and the next.

That does not mean, though, that you cannot reflect upon what has happened. And obviously, we all learn from it. But that does not mean you carry the path on your back as a burden. And it does not mean thinking, "I don't like where I'm at. I want to go over there." That's not the essence of that, either.

No matter what is occurring, it's all occurring in the moment and it's perfect in the moment. It is also appropriate that you plan for the future, look toward the future, but you cannot live in the future. It does not exist. And if you are living in the future, which does not exist, it means that you do not exist.

It is that way in the nonphysical as well. There is nothing but the moment. That is why we have the ability to be in more than one place and one body and more than one existence at one time. We are always in the moment. So the moment exists before us. If you wish to have a mystical look at the way it might be, it's as if we could part the clouds and we see all that there is and it's all spread out in front of us. It's all occurring at the same moment. Because that's all there is.

One of the things that's difficult to understand and you're all doing very well at it, is to understand that there is so much you are seeing from the perspective of what you know intellectually. We are saying there is a different set of eyes where you can see things from the knowing, not from the intellect. You can be wherever you need to be at any given moment.

Time

Why was time created for us?

Because humans wanted some record of their events. Why do you think we came here? We wanted to experience all of this. As we experienced more of the emotions, more of the senses, the feelings, we said, "Oh yes. I feel really good about this and so I wish it to be documented. So I need to have some point in space that says, 'At this moment, I gave myself an award here. I did good.'" And so humans created it.

How do you explain points of time where it feels like you switch to another reality?

Because there is depth to reality.

It's like one moment you're doing this and the next moment you're doing that and you have no idea how you got from here to there.

Those are lapses in time if you will. It is truly that your mind has left the body. It is sort of in a hypnotic state. It is part of what your mind creates for you.

Sometimes things seem to dematerialize or rematerialize. I don't feel like it's a lapse in time.

There is dimension to your existence. What can occur, then, is in the moment you are in, you are in the moment, but you are also in depth. In this moment you can be here in this dimension and you can skip and be into another dimension that mirrors much of this, but things can be changed. It's not as if you've gone backwards and forwards, it's as if you've gone sideways.

Right. I've seen that in Star Trek often. A parallel life.

You know that man had much more going for him than he realized when he was writing these things, this Rodenberry. He was connecting to a much higher realm than the Trekkie fans realized. The man walked with one foot in another dimension. He basically was living the parallel life.

Do not become confused by understanding it. For those who have read books on the fifth dimension, just keep it simple and say it was a singing group in the 60's. Because when you try and define it, you are using your own intellect instead of allowing the knowing to come through. Do not be so locked up in trying to box up and put parameters around these things. Bring the knowledge into your existence instead of making it small by defining it.

There is much to chaos theory. That is truly about how our life and our existence are happening. The same thing does not occur twice. Every time there is a little difference, that is in itself creating and shifting and manifesting it all. So it is very important you are clear not to define things. The moment you define it, it has changed. Because it's energy.

Healing in Time, Healing in Lifetimes

***I** have a question about change then. If you can go sideways, does this open possibilities for healing? For instance, can you go sideways and have some sort of effect in different dimensions that can have some effect in the present by releasing something, an energetic pattern, that goes through the dimensions?*

First, we are saying the word "sideways" simply so that you have a visual of the way it is. The only thing we can say is "dimensional." So, can you heal on more than one level? Absolutely. Over the past number of years, people have defined the dimensions as the energetic levels. The etheric level, the astral level, all these levels.

By defining it, they have shifted it. That's a hard concept so we are going to keep saying it.

These people who have tried to say, "This energetic level is seven" from the body and this one goes out a foot and a half," from our perspective this is not so. But from the human perspective, in order to have something to work with, in order to feel like they are doing something, that definition has worked. Healers have worked at the different energetic levels that have been created. That is the same kind of thing as "yes," healing can occur in dimensional levels as well. They impact and shift.

However, not much work has been done on that, and let us say that any healing that occurs affects all energetic levels, all dimensional levels. The healing that is superficial only works on this dimension.

It is a higher vibration, a pure intent that actually heals at the dimensional level that impacts things. Let us say if there is a deep wound in the skin, you can do healing by putting on an antiseptic, so it is healing on the skin level, but it is not healed at the deep level. There is healing that goes down all the levels.

How about the dimensions that we have as human beings as lives? It's all sideways. It's not progressive. It's all happening at once. I'm asking specifically about going into past lives and that particular dimension.

Let us look at past lives. You have known from your work that when you have someone who is exhibiting some behavior or grief that they are not able to let go of, you take them back to a past life. Perhaps you have to jump back farther and farther, or you go all the way back to the very first existence of it. So you have all the layers and lives that have been affected by it. Or you can go to the source, to the depth of the level and complete it there, shift the energy pattern that shifts all the energy patterns of all the lives and shifts it forward. That mostly works on the emotional illnesses.

Because humans are so connected by emotion, that the emotional illness patterning continues every lifetime. Going back to the source helps it straighten out and become complete all the way through.

Can we look at that issue in terms of souls? Can a soul be living in more than one existence or time period simultaneously?

Yes and they do.

I want to ask about soul retrieval. I had an experience with that last week on two different levels. In my meditative state, I first encountered a child who was six years old who I understood to be me.

In this present life?

Yes. I'm interested to look at it in other lives, too. This time it was a six-year-old and my teenage self that I welcomed back into my soul. It was a profound experience, but I don't know enough about it to understand it.

So it appears to us then, from what we are hearing and sensing, that there are parts of you in this lifetime from different ages that were brought back together and integrated. For us, that does not mean "soul retrieval," but we are understanding that is the terminology that is being used.

What is your terminology?

For this, it's basically integrating all of the different parts of you, emotional parts at the different age groups. What happens in a severely ill person when breaks occur, we do not say severely ill in the same way a medical professional would say it, is that we get those dissociative and split personalities. We all have different ages of development where we are split out emotionally. When a trauma occurs, you have a ray that sticks out of a sphere. What we are seeing is a ball with spines sticking out.

This process has allowed the parts of you that have bulged or poked out to be moved easily and smoothly to become whole. We would call it becoming whole. Integrating all parts of yourself on this level.

For us, soul retrieval is when the soul tries to escape the body. That is very difficult. Sometimes when the soul leaves the body, that is when walk-ins occur. As long as this assists you in your growth, it doesn't matter what you call it. It's as if you are introducing your six-year-old to your twelve-year-old to your thirty-year-old and all of you are getting along at the same place at the same time. Not an easy task.

Now would that affect other parallel lives that she was experiencing because she had these fragments, these spikes? Would now the integration of that personality roll over into the other parallel lives?

To some extent. It all depends. Again, it's like when we think of a wound. Is it a superficial wound or has a deep one occurred? Sometimes one of these spikes is actually pulled out from another dimension because something occurred such as a past life that you're still attached to. And you need to live in this dimension, because that's who you are in this time. This time of no time.

So if it happened in a past life, say at age 35, will they have another crisis in this life at age 35?

Sometimes. Life is so complex, but that is a possibility. Absolutely. That sometimes happens dimensionally. It's like why can a person be perfectly fine and then all of a sudden at age 35 have schizophrenia. Where did that come from? It's possible it came dimensionally through. The other times is that through past lives, they've brought something forward that traumatically happened at that time. It's this way and that way and another way and it's all impacting and pulling and pushing and shoving. No wonder you had so many spikes.

But if you think about it, where else can you play like this? That is the thing that needs to keep being reminded to people. This is play. This is your playground. This is where you get to experiment, try it on, see if it fits, see if the color looks good. It truly is as if you've gone into a clothing store and see this whole rack full of things and you say, "I'm going to try that, and that, and that," and you put this outfit on which is maybe some way of being and you go, "Oh my goodness. What made me think of that?" So you take that off and try something else on.

So if you think of that in terms of relationships, illnesses, connections, all that is occurring to you, you're just trying on outfits.

It seems like throughout my life I've been dealing with souls who keep trying to escape. They don't want to be here. Most of the members of my family were that way, and I was also that way. Is there a way of connecting with those, especially family, who want to leave?

What do you mean by trying to connect with them?

To get them to play the game with you.

There is nothing any one person can do to another person to get them to do anything — especially change. So get that out of your consciousness, unconsciousness, out of your cellular memory. You cannot get anybody to change. Think of how hard it is to make your own self change. And you want to try and make somebody else change? It doesn't work that way and we keep saying this over and over.

The only thing that each one of us can do is to hold a perfect image, space, and energy for another person. That is the only thing you can do for another person. And that is everything you can do for them. What happens, when you hold space and create that energetic space for them, it is a beacon of light. It is absolutely a beacon of light. If someone's out there saying, "I don't know what I want to be or if I want to be," there's always a light there.

And they can go towards that light if they wish to. That light is the image you have held for them in perfection. It's not the image of them you want them to be, it's the image of them in their own perfection, and that is all you can do and everything you can do. You can't make anybody play the game. But you're all out there together. You all said, "Let's try and see if we can do it this time."

I wonder how many times we've all tried to do it.

It's as if you all said, "Baseball didn't work this time. Let's all try playing hockey," and you all got out there with your sticks and said, "This isn't any fun, either." They just haven't found the right game or the right set of rules or equipment. Maybe something more benign next time...

Or shift.

But just because they didn't shift, doesn't mean you aren't. The only one you can change is yourself, and you have. You have changed yourself multiple times. Go back to the show Star Trek and say you are one of those shift-changers.

Shape-shifters.

Those things too, yes.

Can you speak a little bit about when a soul chooses to leave the body, that it isn't because they failed. Not wanting to be on this planet or not wanting to be in this body means they made the wrong decision.

Gladly! There is no such thing as failure. There is really is no such thing as right and wrong in terms of the soul. It is the simple yes and no. Off and on. You are here. You choose not to be here. It's as if you said, "I don't want to do it," and it's okay. Change your course. "I'll try that again later. I'll lose ten pounds and then I'll try it on again."

You came in here to play the game. These truly are your rules. You made them up. You make up the rules every moment of every day. You can say, "Game called on account of rain. Game called because I'm hungry." Or just "I don't want to play anymore." And that's okay. That's the beauty of it because there is lifetime after lifetime after lifetime you can come back and play. "I don't want to play today; I'll play another day." Even those people that commit suicide, even those people who lead very destructive lives and then just leave, it's okay. It's perfect.

It's their game, their life. Life is a game. You make up your own rules. Remember, there is no plan. So what needs to be done in circles like this and other groups is hold space. Hold the intention of the image; the energy that is out there that says no matter what, it is perfect as it is. And if somebody decides at this moment not to be here, that's all it is. They choose not to be here. That's okay because you can come back and do it any day you want to.

This is really a wonderful place to play. So why would someone want to come back into another body and have multiple sclerosis again? The reason is the same reason someone will attempt to climb Mt. Kilimanjaro nine times in a row. Why would you want to climb it once? Every individual soul has its own calling. It's not a matter of asking, "Why would someone do that?" It's simply a matter of, "they do." And it's because they can. That's the only reason. To see if they can, and to play the game.

Now sometimes, it's as if one soul splits. Remember when we talked about cells, and much of the miracle of how the body is created is very similar to the soul and how it's created? It starts as the one and it divides, and divides, and divides. They are all connected to each other and part of the One. We would refer to a twin flame; this is our term for it. A twin soul is one soul divided into two. It's as if twins had been born who are of the same. That's a different thing, where the twin souls are truly seeking the other half of themselves.

That's what you hear many times where a person is in search of their "other half that completes me." Let us not be confused with all of the emotion that goes on with people who meet and after a couple of days, say, "Oh, you complete me." And after six months, say, "Oh, you make me sick." There is that human physical attraction and there is that soul attraction. Two different things. People tend to use the terminology very freely.

Are twin souls both incarnate at the same time?

Not necessarily, and that makes for a miserable being here on the earth. They usually try to, and they usually find each other.

Incarnation: Look to Nature For the Answers

Can you speak to how we decide when to incarnate?

Yes. Because there is no such thing as time, for the most part there is no such thing as hurry. When the soul decides, I'd like to play a game again; you must get the true perspective of things. In a nonphysical existence, it could take 200 years to make that decision, and those 200 years feels as if it's a blink of an eye. So, for us here in the bodies, it is difficult to imagine that length of time when it is only measured on earth. It's truly as if it's only a blink of an eye, and "Oh, I'm ready to play the game."

We have talked before about the vibration increasing and the need for souls to be returning. It's not that there's a time element when they are in the nonphysical. It is a vibrational quickening that is happening that is allowing souls to say, "Oh, it's time to go. I'm moving forward." That's a different thing that is being experienced now because earth energy is vibrating differently.

It's causing everything everywhere to be experienced differently including all those who are in the nonphysical, who are choosing to be the guidance from the nonphysical or choosing to be back on the earth plane so that they can have less forgetting, more remembering, shift the vibration, and change what is happening on the planet.

We don't want you to think we're just sitting back in the rocking chairs on the porch doing nothing. It's not about that. It is truly that there are those in the nonphysical who are really learning, and experiencing, and gathering the knowledge, and working with those in the physical plane. We could say, "How does a seed know when it's time to come up and become a flower?" It's almost as if there just is a knowing.

But it takes the right ingredients.

Correct. It takes the right ingredients. So in the non-physical realm, as things shift and change energetically, all of a sudden, which may take 200 years, all of a sudden the plant decides it's time to grow. It's more than a decision. It's a knowing. The moment is now and all begins to take shape. All the wonders of nature that have been created here on earth are in the image of the soul.

When you look to your answers about the soul, look to nature. That is why there is so much conversation, and worry, and concern about what is being done to nature. Nature is a mirror of the soul's existence. We mean nature in terms of how the body is created, how the mountains and rivers are formed, and in the simplest seed that becomes a plant. The cycle of life that is created naturally is just an image and a mirror reflection of the cycle of the soul.

That also shows the interdependence of all things.

Absolutely. That is why when we destroy nature; we are in essence, destroying our souls. That is why there is that quickening. Why, energetically, everything is raising to a higher vibration. That is why other entities, beings, planets, universes, are watching what is going on. We are destroying ourselves, literally, and figuratively, when we destroy nature.

We can't be alive without plants. There would be no plants, there would be no soil, there would be no air.

There is truly, though, that thing called evolution and things change, and adjust, and move forward. But there is a natural order of that change. Remember as we talked about each one of ourselves individually, we said the only person that can change himself is himself? Likewise, a plant can only change itself. However, we as human beings are creating all kinds of things that are causing changes to happen.

We are destructive to our environment and so the changes that are occurring within our plant life, our soil and our animal life, are a force that they have to adjust to and become something different because of the environment we created. There is a natural order of how they would progress if left alone. Just as each human being and each soul would.

I was reading a book last night that takes that a step further and says that in the process of trying to make everything scientific, we are in the process of destroying ourselves. We are not recognizing the interdependence of everything and as we kill off the rain forest, we are literally choking ourselves.

Yes. When we're killing the rain forest, we are killing ourselves. It's as if for every tree we chop down, we're taking a piece of your finger and cutting it off. If we keep doing it, where will the body be and will it even be a body any longer? Scientists, for the most part, in their zeal to understand, are truly putting everything in boxes. We talked earlier about defining things.

When you define things, you change the order of it. You can't pull those pieces apart because they are connected. It's just as if we had talked about here that we are all connected to each other. You cannot separate each person from the other. To separate yourself is to die. You are connected to everything and everything is connected to you.

Beings from Other Planets: We and They

You spoke of everyone watching and waiting on other universes and planets. Can you speak to the souls that are listening to other places?

Let us be clear that a soul is a soul and it can go anywhere. They may decide, "I don't want to play this game, maybe I'll go to Mars and play that game instead." Earth is the only game that allows for choice and emotion as we know it. We are using the simple words to explain the depth and breadth of this planet. This is the funnest game in town.

Can you tell us what it would be like living on another planet?

We should ask you, you've been there.

I don't remember, unfortunately.

There are just so many different types of existences on planets. There are planets that you go to where it is simply very contemplative, where there is no movement, just thought. Where you are just a thoughtful being. There are planets where you are a vaporous being, with no actual tangible form; where it's just thick molecules, if you want, but no solidness to you.

There are beings on different planets very similar to the beings on Star Trek. Where do you think they get these creations? They think it's their imagination. It's really their past they are remembering. Most of the planets have form and order. You see this is a young planet. Again, when we go back to the no plan and you're creating your plan, earth is creating its existence as it goes forward. Most of the other planets and systems are at a balance. They have created homeostasis. And so there is no real fluctuation. They've found their own nirvana.

For those truly looking for a rest, go to other planets where you can just sit and contemplate your navel for 200 years.

I want to talk about the planets that are only thoughts. Are some of those thoughts things that have come to us that we utilize for scientific achievements or personal developments or that type of thing?

Information that has helped with scientific achievements or progressing the world forward has come from many different places. Many times it's come from the fact that those beings, those personalities such as Albert Einstein, have been able to tap into that which is all-knowing. What happens many times is that people are poking holes in the knowingness and able to draw from the information.

Other times there are interplanetary beings that exist here and other dimensions, and they are the whispers in the ear or the "I wake up one morning and all of a sudden there's something on this paper and I know not where it came from, but it is a phenomenal breakthrough."

Are some of these beings actively helping us in their bodies?

There are some, but there is for the most part, a soul level agreement that says earth is to be left alone in order to be developed on its own. To get back to that, they're really not dropping into the human bodies, that's a no-no, and Captain Picard would slap their hands and they'd be in trouble. More are checking the human progress and are many times doing damage. There's a little too much activity going on with the interplanetary beings pulling humans away and testing them. That really borders on what is not to be done, but it is occurring.

The Path of the Soul

***I**'m not sure about the path of the soul. I don't get the sense that there's an end point, necessarily, or a beginning, or a direct path.*

Let us talk about the soul's path when you come into this life. The most interesting thing is that people are continually thinking that they are here for some magnanimous event to occur. "How do I know my life is successful? How do I know my life hasn't failed? I've got to do something tangible."

Energy is not tangible. You didn't start out tangible. Most of what you are here for, your path, is of the purest and highest nature. You are here to experience and live in joy. Utter and true happiness in your life.

You are here to do what brings passion and fulfillment to you. To experience joy in your life every moment of every day is probably the hardest thing anyone tries to do. And yet it's so simple. If you get out of your own way and quit thinking you have to do something.

It is a state of being that is your path. It is not an accomplishment from doing. You do not set out and say, "My path this lifetime is to create a cure for cancer. My path is to save the world from hunger. My path is to be a terrorist and blow up everybody." Your true path is to experience and live your life in joy. If you are living your life in joy, you are walking softly upon this earth. You are walking hand in hand with this earth, with all that lives here, be it plant, be it mineral, be it animal. That's what the path is. There are many ways you can do that.

But the number one criteria is, "Does it bring me joy?" Because if it doesn't, don't do it. And with that we leave you until our next visit, and we say blessings and *Namaste*.

Living the Life That is Guided

Good evening to you. This is a very sacred day, a time for sacred messages: a time for sacred people to be together. It is no accident that you are here today. The messages that we are to deliver and share are about each other, for each other, and guided by each other. For us today, it is a time of opening. It is a time of inner awareness. It is a time that you be put on notice. From this moment on, your lives will never be the same, although that is always true.

You are part of a sacred inner circle. You know there is no beginning. There is no end. It continues around and around and it goes on forever. You are part of that inner circle of knowingness, connectedness, and being.

It is a time that each one of you to look at your own life and the life you have created for yourself and say to yourself, "From this moment on, I shall not waver. From this moment on, I shall know my path and walk it. From this moment on, there is to be no doubt, no questioning, no 'but what if'." You are all being guided very strongly. Some of you may feel like you are being pushed. Some of you may feel like you are being dragged. Make no mistake, there is much guidance for you today.

The message today is, "How does one lead a life that is truly guided?" You are the examples of those that are being guided. Each one of you has lived, within the last year or two, in fear and in question. We do not mean you have stayed in fear. There has been fear in your life that has said, "What am I doing? Where am I going?" For you have been the ultra-sensitive ones that have known and sensed something bigger and more powerful about you.

You do not have fear of going there, but fear of the unknown. It is the fear that occurs when one questions, instead of knowing. It is the fear that occurs when there is not trust. When you are in trust, entrusted with the truth, then there is a sense of solidity, that "even though I do not know where the road goes, I move down that road. I move down the road in utter faith that where I am going is where I am to be going." Each one of you has said, "I am not clear where I am going. There are moments I feel lost. I am wondering what is going on in my life."

We are here to guide you today, just as your guidance will be the guidance for many. We are here to tell you about the type of guidance available. You are all very, very special people and you each have special paths in life. There will be times you hold each other's hands so you do not feel alone. But know you each have your individual path. Although you walk your paths individually, you are never alone. Individual does not mean alone. It just means singular in what you are specifically doing.

Today is a lesson on trust and believing and faith. It is faith that you have when you sit still with yourself and that inner sense comes welling up from within you and says, "When I get bigger than myself, I have true knowing. I know exactly where I'm going." You are the lighthouse and you must keep your eye on the lighthouse. You create that beacon that you move toward and you are the light that you are moving toward.

One thing that came to me was that if I go to that space between the inhale and the exhale, all I have to do is be willing and available and the rest will happen. Staying in that place is difficult. Do you have a suggestion on how I can remind myself to come back to it?

Every time you feel like you're out of the moment, say, "Come back. You're way out here, come back." What you do then is create a habit. For instance, when you're training dogs and let them too far out on their leash, you say, "Come back. Come back," until pretty soon they're not out on the leash, they're right beside you all the time. All you need to do is shift what you have been "*do*-ing" for all of your life to the way you wish to do and be from now on.

I realize it is be-ing. I also realized another big thing. I thought I had to be ready.

It's not about being ready. It's about being willing. "I allow it. I am willing to be." It is as if the roller coaster has been inching and inching up and the moment that it crests is also the stillness before the motion. Then you have the next crest and the next crest and the next crest. "Oh – now I'm moving out. Now I'm in the moment."

I have some exercises for tai chi and chi gong that I know are good for me and I love doing them, but for some reason it seems hard for me to get started doing them. I don't understand since I've become so joyful doing them. What is it that I need to do to overcome the reluctance?

That is a good point. And how many in here are reluctant to do something that is very good for them? We would say everyone including our Willow. Okay, so there is this little reluctance because right now you are feeling that joy. However, when you are in that misery, are you willing to do it?

Yes.

Ahhh, you see this joy that is occurring much of the time is occurring from the outside. It is not the joy coming from the inside out.

It feels from the inside out.

It's not created on the inside. It's from some other person or being bringing it to you. You see, an internal joy, a joy that comes from being absolutely clear and happy with yourself. A joy you can experience in the midst of a storm. That is what we are wanting to clarify. That joy is coming from the inside as opposed to "there is a man in your life and things are lovely in that way, " kind of external joy.

That actually causes more problems.

We did not wish to say that. Relationships are a challenge sometimes. What causes that reluctance? What are the reasons that people do not do what is good for them?

Laziness. No energy. Afraid of the consequences.

Say more about that.

You might actually be more joyful.

And you would be responsible for creating that, which means then you'd have to be responsible for creating the misery, too.

Another piece for me is it would bring me to all that I am. I would then, minute by minute, be able to tap into that power at will. How do you be there always? The fear is that it will separate me totally.

Separate you from what?

Life as a human.

What if we were to suggest to you that it would make you more human?

I would like that actually. I think there's a bridge that needs to happen.

There is. When you are in the nonphysical you are a spiritual being. You have that connectedness and knowing. When you come on the Earth plane you become a human being. We are all moving toward being a spiritual human being. So do you see if you were to tap into that source in yourself and be connected to your spirit that you could actually be a completely fulfilled spiritual human being? We wish you to try that on for the next week as you would a new hairstyle or pair of shoes. We know that the longer you wear those pair of shoes and think of yourself as a spiritual human being, you will like how that feels and you will want more and more of that. You will want to be the strongest spiritual human you can be because that embraces your body and humanness also. The goal is to be spiritual in your body.

Is there then a huge shift in responsibility with that?

The shift in the responsibility comes in knowing you are responsible for yourself. The shift comes in the fact that "I really am comfortable being responsible for myself." And that is a rare occurrence. Because then there is the knowing that you can create your life, you can manifest, and you can attract all you need to attract. And you can allow things to go away that are no longer needed. And you have power over your life.

We have two camps. We have the camp of people that are still so hooked into their bodies that they have forgotten they are spiritual. All they are noticing is whether it's the pain, or it's the love, or the sex, or the money. "I am so busy doing and feeling all the emotions I can." They are very, very human. Now we have this other group that is trying to be very, very spiritual. They are trying to remove themselves completely from all the humanness by saying, "It's appropriate for me to deny myself because I am on a spiritual path. It is appropriate for me to do without because if I had, then I am not spiritual. So I must study all the different modalities and sacrifice and learn about my goddess, and demons and dark side."

And they're so busy doing that stuff that they forget they're a human being.

What if we take the two camps and create a new one that says, "I am all connectedness. I am connected to my spirit, my higher self, to the higher selves of others, to the source. I have all that I need or want or wish to have. I can create it so that in this body I can do all that I wish to do. What a joyful place to be!" That's having it all. That's having the cake and the frosting and all that goes with it and not gaining an ounce. So we wish for you to try on the new pair of shoes this week and practice being a spiritual human being.

In other words, when you are stuck in being a human, get bigger than yourself and remember you are still spiritual. When you get too spiritual and lofty, get yourself back down in your body.

If we are indeed being pushed or led on our paths, we obviously have sacred contracts with our guides who have agreed to be with us on our paths. Do you have any specific information on how we can access our guides and listen more closely so the path will be clearer?

For each one in this room, there are several things that could occur for you around the clarity. We know that for each one here during your dream state you are busy in your school. There is so much homework that you do not have time to call up your guides and say, "Hello, do you have anything for me?"

Night school?

The unfortunate thing for those of you in this room is you are going to night and day school and taking weekend courses too. For those of you that feel like you have no energy, it is no wonder. We are maxing you out at this time. We are going to suggest that one of the easiest things for you to do is to sit with a paper and pencil and allow guidance to write for you.

You suggest a pencil versus a computer?

You're just sitting there saying, "Hey guides, got a message for me?" And let it write and be amazed at what comes out for you. That takes no effort for you. Pen, paper, keyboard, whatever works easiest for you.

I assume that also works in other things I have to write.

Absolutely. And for some of you, there's a block that says, "What if nothing comes?" Because it's a task you're trying to accomplish. In this there's no task. It's like dialing up a guide and saying, "Hello? Are you there?" Maybe instead of CNN, we can have a GNN? (Guided Network News!)

That's why dreams are not working.

Right. You are way too busy. We know you are feeling as if, "I have no choice." Although, you really do have a choice. It's like you are the snowball and you are rolling down the hill. There's no way you'll stop the snowball until the snowball stops. Just enjoy the ride.

We know because you are moving so fast and feeling this guidance, you really did set up these contracts before you came into the physicalness. You have set up certain things.

Each of you said, "There are things I am moving forward to do." And you set it up with guidance saying, "I'm going to need your assistance, because there will be times I'll take a left turn instead of a right. I need for someone to put up the detour signs and get me back on course." The tug and the pull is not only your higher self, it's also your guides saying, "Wake up. Wake up.," in order to keep you moving forward.

Also, it's the urgency of the vibration of the planet. You are amassing all of your own energies and sources and you are becoming a powerful being. That is partly another reason you are feeling so tired. Not only are you attracting that which you need, but you are letting go of stuff that no longer works for you. That is an energetic process. Your bodies are sometimes moaning and groaning. You may have aches and pains where you didn't before. The energy is moving around so that you only have that pure source of energy you'll need to move forward these next 20-25 years. It's not the next 18 months.

How can I move forward when I'm stuck behind a pile of things I don't want to do?

Use one of your newfound vocabulary words. It's a big word, a most scientific word. It's the biggest word in the English language, perhaps in all the languages, and it is one word that all of you must incorporate and embrace and that word is "No." The two most powerful letters which, when put together, allow you to do what you want to do and wish to do, as opposed to what others want you to do. Say "no" to them and "yes" to yourself.

You have a very good and kind heart. You are always helping others to the detriment of yourself. It's partly because there were many times in your life you felt no one was there to help you. You did not want others to go through what you've gone through. There comes a time when you need to say, "I am ready to say yes to all who are standing by to truly help me." And open your arms up and let them in as opposed to putting them across your chest and saying, "I am so determined! I'm going to do it no matter what."

Because when you cross your arms and hold them tight, you not only hide the light, you squish your heart and your will and your energy. You keep it so tightly bound up. Because you have so much energy and so much to give and it can't get out, it takes form in your body and causes it much pain. If you allow your arms to open up, if you allow your beacon to shine out, then the energy within you has somewhere to go as opposed to sitting in your wrists or shoulders or neck where you feel like you've got the weight of the world on you. Or it's sitting in your other organs that are just trying to survive because they feel so constricted.

It is time for you to be all that you are. Not just a part of who you are. You have much to give to this world. It's not about giving up yourself any longer. It's about giving that which you know and have to share. It's sharing, not sacrificing. Okay?

There's a second part to that too. Allow others to give to you.

You see today we're getting at how you can be all you signed up to be. Willow has this story about her mother. She could never tell her mother, "But I never asked to be born!" Because her mother always told her, "Oh yes you did!" So guess what? You asked for this. You wanted this. And the world needs all that you have to give. It's no accident. You are putting out a lot of energy in a lot of different ways and it needs to be focused. The energy needs to be focused, but to be focused you need a bigger box. The box needs to be larger in terms of what you need to do.

I get that message very clearly this week.

Good. As your vision becomes clearer about what you have to offer and how you can offer that, then the energy gets focused in it. As your vision gets larger, the focus gets narrower. Opening up and allowing instead of trying to cause things to happen. In your quiet time you're asking for an answer to a question. How about allowing what needs to come, come. You need to be in the bigger picture. Allow the bigger picture and information to show up, about who you are, how you do things. The more often you write, the more clarity will come.

Can you suggest ways for me to let go of the past and move forward into this new future you talk about?

Create for yourself a ceremony. Take yourself on a hike. Write about all your past experiences. Put on paper all the things you're afraid of; all the things that are stuck in your cells and memories and burn them up. Use fire to help you release things that no longer serve you.

The new moon is a very important time for each of you. You must do a ceremony on the next new moon and play your instrument and create a ceremony around new creations of life, of direction, and honor the four directions. This is for you to create within yourself all that you have within yourself. Within the next seven days create a ceremony to burn away the fears and those memories that are keeping you from moving forward. When you come to the new moon, have a ceremony that creates all newness in your life. We suggest that perhaps every day you create a small altar and light a candle and say, "I burn away all that is old, all that no longer serves me around this issue." You light a match and release it from all your soul, all your memory, and all your energy.

There are two things to do: one is the burning away of the old. The other is celebrating the new on the new moon. You must go forward with that which does not make sense because that is what is moving you forward. And you must do it with joy.

Yes, it's hard.

The messages you receive about your direction in life are those that cause a physical reaction in your body. They are putting you back in the place where your biggest fears and humanesses have occurred. Your path now is to be a spiritual being, in your human body. In order to do that you must let go of that which is attached to the human body: that past history energy. We suggest you gather people that want to bang their drums and blow their horns and help you create a release for yourself.

No matter where your paths take each of you, the connections shall never be undone.

It seems like how I am in the world is what's important, and what I do is insignificant and may change week by week, day by day, year by year.

You are absolutely clear. Who you are in the world is all that matters. Because each of you has a special message, gift, or talent to share in the world, you are each struggling in how to deliver the message. Each of you is clear about your own message. What is the most important thing is that you walk and talk your message. Be it until the mechanism unfolds. With each other's help, it will become clearer and clearer every moment. Clarity will come to each of you. You will each know exactly what you're doing and where you're going. And the year after that it will change. But do not despair. Each level will unfold, one after the other. The unfoldings may be a matter of days or weeks or months or years but you will continue to open and know. It is only the mechanism, or the "but how?" you are seeking now. You can sleep easier tonight. No matter what you are doing, as long as you are your message.

You are being what you agreed to be. So at this time we wish to say, "Go with God. Go with Love, and go with each other." *Namaste*.

Abundance

Everything is energy and what is going on for you at this point is unlearning what you have spent a lifetime reinforcing. It is a matter of simply shifting a thought and it's all changed. However, shifting a thought when you have had a multitude of thoughts over your lifetime going in one direction can be difficult to maintain. We are here today to say it is absolutely imperative that all of you, individually and collectively, stand firmly grounded in the energy of the earth. Grounded in the intention that things are perfect as they are.

We know that it is difficult to imagine at three a.m. that all is perfect when you are not sleeping. Or when the bill comes in and the checking account says you have $50 and the bill is $150.

Holding the space for the energy to manifest itself and saying it is perfect as it is, does work out. As each one of you individually ramps up your energetic vibration, as you open up to possibility, as you expand in your knowledge and awareness, sometimes you expand so quickly, there's this space in between that feels like a void. It's scary and you're waiting for yourself to catch up with where you're moving.

First, it's no accident that you are here together. If you were doing your stuff by yourself, it would be a much scarier place. The whole key to moving forward is that you have each other. Even if there is no conversation going on between you, you carry each other's energy. You are holding the energy of the group and you are holding the energy for those that are not here as well. Even the non-physicals are still part of us.

What we wish to do today is clarify any questions. If you have any questions specifically about the nature of what is going on for yourself in this moment, we would like to be of assistance in moving forward. We remember, in its simplest form, that each of you are being asked to take each negative particle, be it thought, atom, or ion, and just flip it. It's the coin. Flip it over. It's the switch. Flip the switch. Take the dark and create light. It is making the shift from no to yes.

For every thought you have, it must be shifted into that positive shift. You are creating new habits, a different way of walking and talking and most importantly you are creating a different way of thinking. You are creating that way of intention, positive intention only. So you can absolutely sit here and say, "There is not enough money in the moment in my checkbook to pay my bill, but that does not mean there is not enough money." Do you understand?

To say in the moment, "I am not able to pay my bill" is a statement. But when it is "I am not able to pay my bill and I do not know where the money will come from and I'm very worried about it," all of those are all the little negatives around it. When you make a statement make it factual. Matter of fact.

However, that does not mean there isn't enough money. Do you get the difference? We are speaking of money because you come from a society, a background, and lives where that has become very important to you. We know that is not the most important thing in your lives or you wouldn't be here. But there is an importance of it. We are absolutely and clearly saying it is simply a matter of changing the intention, of holding a pure image of whatever is needing to be fulfilled in your life. Hold that the highest and best good will happen for you.

Physical and Non-Physical Energy

I want to ask about energy, physical versus nonphysical. What is the difference between the physical and nonphysical?

Actually, there is no difference. As we have said many, many times in our channelings, the only difference between you and I is that one is physical, actually able to be seen by all people, and the nonphysical are only able to be seen by certain people. We all have the same sense. It is truly as if we are all the same energy. Some are just denser than others. Therefore, they become physical. In the nonphysical state, we are capable of connecting to the energy and information and soul easier than those in the physical state.

Remember, those spirits that came into the physical body chose to do so to experience different things; emotions, choice, and free will, and through lifetimes have chosen to forget all they knew before they came in. Those are the differences. We do not wish to infer anything to this group, but physicals are more dense.

When things come through a channel, is there an opening up of something that enables that to occur?

How does one channel then? There are several ways it is done. We have spoken of the spirit, the part of the soul that now enters into the body and integrates with the personality. When the consciousness of the physical one is put to sleep in a deep trance channel, the spirits inter-join with the spirit of the physical so there isa co-mingling of the energy. That is why many times the channel has a discomfort of the body. There is a sense that there is not enough room. Or the body has to stretch or get larger and sometimes the non-physical takes far too much energy of the physical one in order to do the channeling.

Willow does it a different way. She always does things differently. It is not that a second spirit drops down and co-mingles with her spirit in the body. It is as if her spirit, her essence rises up to and merges with *The Band*. The energy depletion she feels is because she is needing to move her body to raise up to the vibration as opposed to letting something drop down into her body. We really hate to say up and down because there is no up and down.

I just have an intuitive sense of Willow's energy extending away from herself in certain directions that are causing discomfort.

This is the way she learned to be an intuitive and a channel. She goes out and seeks the energy of others to read them, as opposed to keeping the energy where it belongs, in her body, and letting someone come close to her so she can read it and then letting them go back. She's always out there in everybody's bodies. As a result, the energy in her solar plexus is so intense that she blows it out her back. She refers to it as a sick back. She feels a pain in her back that feels nauseous. She has experienced that for many, many years.

Every once in a while someone will ask me a question, and I'm listening as carefully as they

are because I don't know what the words will be until they're said. Is that also channeling?

You could call almost anything channeling. What you are absolutely doing is tuning into the right radio station. You are being asked a question and you are seeking the answer from your Higher Self or from other records, and allowing that information to come in. There's a difference. When you are channeling, you are literally having an entity, or a group, use your body to come forth with the information. More of what you are doing is using your intuition to tune into the right place for that knowledge, and letting the faucet pour out without it having to regurgitate in your mind.

The World at Large

Good evening to you our dearest friends. It is a special time, a time of true connectedness, of almost worship, a time to be here with each other and with those who could not be here. It is a time to be aware, to open up, to be bigger than all that is going on in our lives and in the lives of others.

There is a solemnity about us today. There is a seriousness that we wish to move forward into. But as serious as we can be, there will still be a time or two for a little joke. But we are putting on our special serious hat. We really wish to acknowledge all that is going on in the world and our communities today, and put some perspective on that in terms of time. It is the perfect time. And yet the perfect time means there is no time at all because it is all in the moment.

How will the elections impact the world and our lives? Is there some divine plan about it all?

If we can all put our mindsets around that and how we are going to live our lives in perfection and with the intention that all is well as it is, then we will proceed.

It is a time of struggle and a time of great ease. It is a time when each one of you decides whether you wish to be in the way of being that is struggling or the being that all is well and in its perfection. That is a choice each person needs to make. It is a choice most people don't understand they have to make. We can see some of the horrendous things that are going on in the world and bless those events and know that from those events there is much learning that is occurring. It is not sacrifice. It is moving forward. It is allowing things to unfold.

If you step into the center of the unfolding, then you are in the center of the flower of which all life occurs. Of which all things too shall pass. In death occurs life;

in life occurs death. It is all part of the circle. All part of *The Band*.

I wish to know more about energy. In some way energy is all alike, all from the same source and yet it's divided down. When it gets divided into thoughts, actions, beliefs and so forth, does it take on different qualities?

Good question. Yes, energy is energy. As it comes from the one source, it is all pure, and all the same. Now if you were to take two masses, two rocks, one of gold and one of coal, you'll find the amount of energy that is in a dense piece like gold has different properties to it on the exterior and in the way it behaves. Coal has its own unique properties. The reason the energy seems different and appropriately acts differently is because of the mass of the energy that is together within it. It is how tightly compacted the energy is. It's not how tightly compacted, tightly knit the essence is, but how tightly the energy is within it that creates different properties.

For instance, if you have molecules floating around and they are not very densely collected together, you could almost say it is a scattered thought. As thought formulates, it causes energy molecules to be attracted to each other, and become more and more focused or aligned with each other. The spaces between them that allow for a different sense of properties are removed from it, so what we are getting is the purest essence of the energy with no room for all the discordance. The more someone is focused, the less space there is and the more it is filled up with this pure energy.

In general, would actions be more dense than thoughts?

Yes. A thought creates an action. Many times if the thought is clear, pure, and focused, then the thought is more dense. If the thought is not pure enough, then the action that occurs it is more diluted. When you have an action and a thought that are in alignment with each other as in karate, then there is a pureness of thought and the energy is purely formed and the hand or head can break the bricks. There is no room for the space in between.

How do you know when your thought is focused enough?

It is that moment between the inhale and the exhale. It is the moment between night and day. It is for most human beings a practiced art. How do you get to that place? Practice and more practice. It is continually practicing and focusing your complete thought on something. The other way to get there is totally let go and allow it happen. You are the most focused when you let go.

In biofeedback, often there are no words for the state you need to be in to have something happen. If you will it to happen, it doesn't happen.

Correct. So the most focused you will ever be in your life is when you are not trying to be focused. It is in the state of being when the most focused doing occurs.

It sounds hard. The one advantage of biofeedback is the equipment tells you when you're in the state so then you can tap into yourself and say, "Oh, I'm doing what I need to be doing right now."

Correct. For those in the beginning stages of learning, biofeedback is very useful. However for those in this room and those who are opening up to all that is, it is a matter of meditating. That is where you begin to find that state. We believe every single person in this room has gotten to that state where there is such a stillness that you know that everything is occurring, and nothing is. When you let go of it all in order to have everything, you are in the state of pure meditation. That moment in your quiet meditation is the moment when you can manifest, when action has the most energy, when you have the most clarity and pureness of thought, and a knowingness of things you did not know before. It is that moment that you know you have the skill and ability to do anything your mind can possibly come up with.

How do energy and intent interact? I believe when you have 100% intent, that is the focus you're speaking about. When whatever the intent is manifests immediately.

Okay. We have spoken about the pure energy vibration you can have by letting go. Intent and energy go hand in hand. You are intending the energy and the energy is the intent. They are one and the same. What we were learning and remembering when we were working on our abundance was the fact that when you put out the picture of what you are wanting, you need clarity around the intention. Clarity gives you the utmost focus. It gives you your intention. Specific direction. Without clarity, your intention becomes scattered.

I am still a little confused about the role of emotion in all of this.

The role of emotion could be the first line in a book, "How to be scattered in ten easy lessons." Emotion is that which scatters the energy. That is the challenge of being here on this earth plane, of being here in this body. We must all think of this as a joyful exercise. We came here to say, "I knew when I did not have a physical body, that I could have clarity of intention and it could occur. Now I want to play with my emotions and experience all of this and see if I can still do it." Got that? This is the only and every game in town.

The more we get you to understand that this is playing, and we do not mean playing to the extent that we are harmful to others or lacking respect; that when you are so intent on the playing, and the joy, and the fun, and the experience, and the exchange, your emotions and intention are in perfect alignment.

However, we all came here with all the challenges; the worry, the fear, the anger, the frustration. Think about this. What if you could have the most exquisite meal you could think of, and eat it three times a day, every day of the week, 52 weeks of the year, year after year after year? This wouldn't be so much fun. You'd get bored. So, instead you go out and say, "And then I'm going to a restaurant and have a fast-food hamburger. And then I'm going to try liver and onions, and all kinds of other foods because I know what my perfect meal is and I know I can have it any time I want it." I just want to try other meals. The problem is, we forget what the perfect meal is and that we can have it any time we want it. So we begin to believe that our meals are only junk food.

Keeping with the food analogy, imagine going to our refrigerator, which might be a symbol of your emotional baggage, and all you see is cheese with mold on it, and turkey that's outdated, milk that's going to spoil and leftovers you're not interested in eating, and then you think, "I can't find anything to eat." And that refrigerator is all your emotion all bagged into one. And you believe that that's all there is in life. All you need to say is, "I can think of that perfect meal, and I can eat it and I won't gain one ounce on my body. It will be perfectly processed every time I want to eat it. And that includes all the chocolate cake I wish to have. And I can have that whenever I want it."

We are here to have a smorgasbord, to experience all of our emotions. However, we forgot that we can have our favorite meal every time we want it. Not any time, but every time. And that favorite meal is joy. And that favorite meal is walking a path of happiness. That favorite meal is what gets you up in the morning with a song in your heart, keeps a smile on your face all day, and allows you to go to sleep saying, "I've had the most perfect day, and I love being alive!"

If you were having that day, you could create and manifest anything because your intention and emotion would be pure and in complete alignment with each other. You could say, "It's all possible." All I need to do is put it out there and it's there." That's how emotion works with our energy.

Could you speak to how larger forces are impacting us as we are starting to stay clear with our intention and hold our own emotions that are

so obviously affected by big stuff going on in the world?

First we wish to say to you, honor your emotions. Honor the piece of moldy cheese in your refrigerator. You could cut that off and it's still good cheese. Honor your emotions. Do not try to hide them, suppress them, pretend they don't exist, because they do and it's what you came here to experience, and it makes up who you are.

The issue is, do you let those emotions lead your life? Or do you let Life lead you? So, what is most important is number one, honor your emotions, and appreciate the fact that there is anger, or sadness, or fear in your body, but do not allow it to guide your life. What you must do then is find what in your life brings you joy. When you tap into that energy, you tap into the one source. You get yourself hooked back in. That is the quickest way to hook back into source.

Get yourself back into the space that you know and feel is your life connected to joy.

The forces, i.e., people, governments, are not some ominous evil force, but manmade forces, are tugging at those emotions of yours that stir up the fear, that cause each of you to question who you are and if you're doing the right thing. They cause you to have the sense of being lost, of having no choice, or the sense that there is no hope. They hook into that and then they pull you. There are many unhappy, desperate people in this world who are unable to remember the joy to hook into. Some of those people choose to cause terror and fear in the lives of others. There is a portion of that going on. There is also a portion of souls that are here that have made agreements with each other that say, "I'll help you with your growth." And sometimes growth comes from what we perceive as terrible events. If you can know that in the Universal Soul Sense, that all things are moving back toward the One, if you can hold onto that thought and feeling, then there is a sense of "it is all right in its perfect time."

Let us go with your political scene. You are not long from elections, which will have tremendous impacts on this country and where it will be headed. Beheaded. Interesting. Even we have Freudians up here.

What is being played out right now is: "Can we hook people into fear? Or can people remember joy in a world where we want to live?" That is at stake right now. There is a tug between keeping people in fear with blinders on so people can no longer see, and are we going to take the blinders off so we can see and make choices. You can make informed decisions, not based on emotion, but on life, on truth. Decisions that will forward the planet. It is imperative that each one of you here, and all you touch, do not go to a place of fear with the elections, but of trust that all will turn out for the highest good. Your current government is trying to get people to believe, if you're not for us, you're against us. If you're not for us, you're against your country. Do not go there. Hold fast your belief in goodness, in truth, in joy. Hook into joy. Hook into the one source and know that all is evolving perfectly.

I just want to make an observation. It's hard to look at forward movement, if you're thinking of being in the moment. That confuses me and takes me back to side issues. I am starting to get more of a picture of trajectories.

Let us see if we can create a picture where you can understand movement as we speak of it. A flower, which grows in the ground and starts with a bud, has movement when its petals begin to unfold and it begins to open up. But the flower hasn't gone anywhere. So it's all moment to moment. So when we are talking about movement, we are talking about unfolding, and opening and being fully present to all that is. That occurs in the moment and in the moment and in the moment and in the moment.

Your life is made up of millions and millions of moments, but not minutes and hours.

When you begin school and first have to learn your numbers and then you learn how to put them together and how to take them apart, and then you learn how to create more numbers and you create more and more until you get into complex things. That is where we are going. We needed to understand the numbers first. As this group evolves, then we can go into the deeper and deeper understanding of time and no time and moments. But the foundation needed to be laid first.

I would also like to ask how the E.T.'s and other life forms are impacting the world?

It is very interesting. In our conversations in this material, we're not going to go dimensionally because there are beings of many dimensions. On a simple level we wish to say, all entities come from the one source regardless of where they live. Of course they live the same way you humans do. There has been an agreement that this planet earth is to be observed, and not manipulated and shifted. Truly the earth is not an experiment, it is an idea that is being allowed to unfold. The beings and spirits that come here are creating the plan as they go along. So those beings that choose not to be embodied here on the earth plane, are truly holding the space that all will unfold, as it needs to unfold. There are energetic watchings that are going on.

There are those that are curious. There are E.T.s, if you will, that have many times used human bodies to check on evolution. There are also things that happen to the human bodies that are expelled into the universe that impacts the "E.T.s. It is an agreement to allow the earth to be what it is to be, and there are those that are holding space for a higher intention and creating a benign energy so they are neither pushing nor pulling, but allowing energy to be used as it needs to be used.

So if someone of free will invites them to participate, is that not allowed?

It depends upon what they're invited to participate in. Should they be invited to a little ceremonial circle, to wear YaYa Hats, I don't know if anyone is interested in that but you never can tell. There are those that sit in anticipation of a connection. And we have a sense that you would wish to be one. You'd like to be contacted or connected. So if you are to be out on a full moon in your back yard and somebody shows up, it's going to impact your life for the rest of your life and all those you tell. Should they be captured and a lot of rigmarole goes around that that makes a lot more impact than showing up for a late night barbecue.

Were you talking about substances within our body which were being expelled into the atmosphere? Could you say more about that?

There are a lot of energies. As you pick up energies from a lot of substances created within your environment, it is absorbed into your body and your body changes and readjusts and shifts. There is stuff leaving your body all the time. Chemicals. Chemicals have come into your body over the generations. Those that come into your body are expelled into the Universe. As your body is shifting and changing so is the atmosphere, so is everything else that is above. These experimenters are checking to see how your body is growing, changing. They are more like guardians of the universe. They are making sure that what is coming out of your body is not going to harm others outside the sphere of human influence.

What do they do with people who have harmful substances coming out from them?

It's not a matter of it happening to an individual. It's a matter of this is happening to the human race.

Are you talking about free radicals?

It's much more complicated. There are subatomic particles coming out that have not even been discovered by your scientists. There is much that is being spewed out into the atmospheres. Even if it's not coming through the skin, it's coming through elimination, or respiration and many different sources. The bodies are being tested to see what is happing with different organs and how are they being able to handle all the impurities that are coming into the human body.

Is there such a thing as evolution? You're implying from what you just talked about that there is, but I'm not sure what your answer would be, so maybe you could speak to that — evolution.

There are at least two different kinds of evolution. One is how does the human body evolve based on your time, the changes in culture, atmosphere. There is a physical evolution that occurs. There is also a spiritual evolution occurring. That is really what we're focusing on. Allow the E.T.'s to mind the store in terms of the physical. The bodies are evolving. The only reason your body dies is because your mind thinks it's going to die. The only reason your body gets old---and all you need to think about this one---is became you believe it is so.

Generations believe that when you reach forty certain things occur, and when you reach fifty other things occur, and by the time you're eighty your body is no longer functioning, That is only a belief, but a very strong one. It is an intention that has come down through centuries and centuries of believing. But have you noticed that all people are living longer and healthier lives? Even skin tone and face are staying younger longer. And we're not talking about all the tucks and lifts and botoxes.

The body in general is able to live longer because there is a belief you're going to live longer. So what we truly wish to impart is there will come a generation where you have a body until you tire of that body and then you will create another body. You do not have to recycle. The body can recycle but the spirit can stay here.

Sometimes it seems exhausting to think of starting all over again as a baby and having to go through a whole life to get to the point where you may have left off and really meant to finish and didn't do it that time. That's a lot of work.

That is true. Perhaps you can create a sort of body-creating machine, saying "I want to start off at twenty years old knowing all that I know and just plop yourself into a twenty year old body."

That's not the way it works right now. Except for walk-ins. But how often do they occur as opposed to regular reincarnation theoretically?

Walk-ins are occurring more and more because it takes too long to go from being a baby when assistance and knowledge and connections are needed now. This is occurring on a more rapid rate. Let's say a Mary is not being able to work through what she thought she'd be working through in this lifetime and there's a Joan who can use the body and make steps forward for what is needed, so it's happening more. So there's a lot more agreements and moving in and out. If your spirit decides that it no longer chooses to go forward this lifetime, that doesn't mean the body has to die. That means the body can be used by another spirit that has work that can be done right now, today.

Let me pose you a major challenge. If you have someone who sees no other way in his life, like this unfortunate angry person who shot the people this week, why couldn't he just move on and let someone who could use the body show up?

Part of it was the agreement he made between himself and the people who were shot. They were actually helping him to evolve. Now why didn't somebody walk in? Because he was not an aware of that. There was a situation that needed to be played out. Walk-ins do not often occur with suicidal people. They occur at times with people who have completed what they came here to do. Their body is still vital, usable, and so that occurs more.

What about the potential of being able to evolve far enough to keep the body and keep rejuvenating it as I've heard some avatars do?

It is occurring now. You're not seeing it on the cover of Time magazine though. There are human beings on this earth that are not aging and are continuing to replenish their body. That is right now the exception. We are sharing with you that that is really the rule.

The potential is there.

Absolutely.

I'd like to go back to that earlier part about having pure intention. What more would you

say to us about holding that energy and being in that joy? How can you help us be there?

In order to be there, find the simple things in life. If you want a task, think about your own life. Perhaps in your quiet time, make a list of five or ten things that guarantee bringing a grin to your face. What is it in your life that causes your heart to sing? It is the opening of the door and seeing the sunrise. It is perhaps a walk in the canyon and seeing the deer. Perhaps it is seeing the first little sprout from plants you have planted. Make that list and know what those things are, and connect with that feeling. That is the feeling you want to pull into your life always.

When you see that glorious sunrise or sunset on the mountains and you realize how magnificent life is, how phenomenal and glorious this world is, that's the energy you pull in. That's the intention. It's getting yourself bigger than your problems. Sunrise and sunset and a puppy dog on your bed or the sound of your favorite music, or the feeling you get when you're kind to a stranger, all those are the most important things in life. That's the energy you need to focus on.

That's the feeling you need to feel when the mortgage comes and you're wondering how you'll pay it. Sit back and get big about your life. Getting big about your life is about becoming very, very simple. Ask yourself, "What makes my heart sing? What brings a smile to my face and joy to my life?"

Would you explain the gravity of the soul and how that relates to existence in the nonphysical and the physical?

It goes back to the emotions. Once the spirit is reunited with the soul and is back in its One state, it has within it the memories of all the personalities and the connection to the life that it just departed from. It has the memory of the emotion and the loved ones and the life it led. Part of the soul's work might be assisting in the growth of those left behind; assisting in the unfolding of the life, the moving forward. Helping the people left behind so they do not get stuck in the grief. The emotions of those grieving on the earth plane saying, " I miss my loved one. I cannot go on. Is my loved one okay?" are like emotional cords that go up (and we're being metaphorical because there's not an up or a down). Those cords are the gravity that hold that soul and says, "These people are still needing to be helped." It's literally a force like gravity.

Friends have asked me on more than one occasion what causes a spirit or entity to want to hang around on this earth plane. I can't imagine and neither can she, once you're released from your body, why you'd want to hang around talking to everybody all the time. The answer is: the gravity of the soul. In other words, what holds the soul to the earth plane is the emotional energy of those people that are here. It is our emotion that hooks onto them. They let go of the emotion. They have the memory of the emotion. But they don't actually continue to have that feeling like we do.

It's our emotional energy cords that are hooking them in and they say, "Oh what the heck?" Up there, it's not even a blink of an eye. "I can be connecting to this person here that's wanting to find out I'm okay. And at the same time I'm in another incarnation talking to them."

Male vs. Female Energy

At the end of WWII, the baby boom started. The reason so many women were born then is because at that time, the country, and the world, and the people felt the possibility that the entire planet would be annihilated through wars. If the world proceeded the same way, dominated by men, it would become extinct because they would destroy us through wars. A large group of souls said, "What is needed on this planet is the female energy such that we can cause peace and return the balance that is needed."

If you think about what happened after WWII, a few years of peace, then the Korean War and a few years of peace, then the Vietnam War. Men have tried to resurge their power by creating new wars. All they've managed to do are the little ones. We refer to little ones as shorter in duration. Granada. The Gulf War. Even during the 60's and the peace movement, there was a tide of feminine energy returning. What's happening now is there is this last ditch effort by male energy to take over again.

We are being called to stand in our own true power and energy and not allow that which is trying to be moved forward with male energy. That is why our feminine energy and the knowledge and information we have are becoming clearer and more connected. Those that are being called to step forward are almost not being given a choice.

Is that why some of us are dealing with such male-dominated energy?

Absolutely. There are so many places where women are swimming against incredible odds in male-dominated environments. So there needs to be a return to balance. Just as the male energy is trying to resurge, the female energy is trying to take control. Those of us who are living in more male and female balance are being called forward. A totally female-dominated world is just as bad as a totally male-dominated world.

It feels like a salmon going upstream when you work with 95% male energy.

We're here because we have the balance. We're clear about the softness, connection, and tenderness and then, we feel this huge push, which is our male energy saying, "Get out there and do it!" and then the female energy saying, "It all has to fit and be harmonious." It's the struggle going on with us to find the balance within ourselves. It's not about us being here as feminine. It's about us being balanced women and attracting balanced men into our lives and circles and beliefs and all that we do. Many of the balanced men are typically gay. The gay men who are not afraid of the feminine and those men who can stand strongly as gay men, are the men that are balanced.

I heard someone say those are the most mature souls of the planet, those who are willing to come and do that.

I don't get the sense of the most mature.

But they're courageous.

There's a willingness to do all that it takes to move the planet forward. Our planet assists in moving the whole Universe forward. We are unique. Everyone is watching us. Everyone is sitting on the bleachers, cheering us on. That's why they're contacting you---those alien guys. It's easier to contact you. They want to help too. They're like the cheerleaders and want to give you any information that will help. When we talk about holding the space and being the lighthouse, that's what we're here for.

But it's not a neutral position, by any stretch. It's first finding the balance and moving forward and bringing others with us from a position of balance.

Think about the earth in perfect balance. When we talk about balance, think of this, when you're breathing, you're connecting in from the earth energy, pulling it up into your higher self and bringing it back down. That's perfect balance. The moment between light and dark, night and day, the moment between yin and yang, where everything occurs and nothing occurs. The perfect balance. The good "evening."

Being in the Flow

I've been going through a tremendous amount of healing. Is everything going to be okay? Should I continue to put energy into the work I'm doing?

We have heard 'shoulds' in the questions. The question each one of you has to ask from this moment out is, "Does this bring me joy? Does this make my life fuller?" What do you want to do with the proposal? Think about this. When you are doing things in joy, they are effortless. You are in the flow. When you're in the boat, you don't have to do anything; you just have to float.

It's a matter of knowing if you're in the boat or not.

And which boat you're going in. Some of you are trying to get in the speedboat here. When you are in the boat, it's the same river. It's still going in the same direction. It's okay to get in different boat.

What keeps coming up is how much negative thinking is still in my being.

How wonderful to be aware of it! Now you can let it go.

You will never be given more than you can handle. When you are sitting before a feast at the table and you have your plate and you start picking at food, or someone plops something on your plate, pretty soon your plate is full so that you need to start taking things off of it. When the plate is full you can take things off. It doesn't mean the only way to take things off is shove them in your mouth because then you're sick from all the things you ate.

Your plate, your life, what you are doing, only has this much room, and you can pick and choose what you want. You can take a bite and say, "This doesn't taste good any longer. I used to like this, but I don't any longer," And you take it off your plate. You don't have to leave it on your plate simply because it's there or someone gave it to you.

You don't know how to say, "No thank you." This is the time for saying, "This is what I want. This is what I need. This is what I'm choosing to experience." And the rest of it, scrape off your plate. When we say, "You are never given more than you can handle," it means when you are given more, get rid of something. You don't have to handle it all. This is important for each of you to remember. You are all very caring, nurturing and giving individuals. It's what your lives have been about —giving to others. From this moment forward, your new mantra is, "If I don't give to myself first, I can't give to others." That is being smart, not selfish.

Consider yourself as a car, a vehicle, a jeep, whatever you'd like. Unless you put gas in your tank, you'll only go a certain distance. No matter how many people you promised rides to, if there's no gas in the tank, none of you are going anywhere.

This is your year for clarity, for absolutely knowing what it is you want and can give and are willing to give.

You must start saying no so you can start saying yes to yourself. Saying yes to yourself means you are saying yes to the life you have chosen and are becoming part of. We are just providing you with the guidelines, the roadmap, and the rules of the road.

I'm just beginning to get an image of the big picture. It's obvious to me there are at least five different boats I can get into. There are a lot of different things I can do and a lot of different deadlines. I'm trying to decide which boat to get in.

Think about this. Sometimes there are boats that are just right next to each other. In order to get to the boat over here, you need to climb through the other boat. Sometimes getting into the next boat is simply so you can get into the boat on the other side of that one. The most important thing is don't have one leg on one boat and the other on the other boat. Sometimes it's just easier to jump in the boat. Don't straddle it. Either you jump or you're being hauled into it.

I'm being hauled into it.

There's no time for hesitation. There's no time for reluctance. There's no time. Allow yourself to step back from it. What happens a lot of times is that you get into this boat, this project, and you get yourself so involved. You need to step back and say, "What is the most important thing I need to get from that?" This stepping back is your meditation. It is a focused meditation. I need to ask clearly for my guidance to say, "What is the most important thing that I need to be learning and experiencing from this?"

Having deadlines is probably good. That limits the amount of time I can spend on something.

The next question is, "Is this deadline realistic or am I imposing it on myself and making my life difficult and I'm out of joy, or is this something that gets me moving so I can accomplish what I want?" A lot of us feel in order to get something done we need to feel some pain. This is not so any longer. Sometimes when you cannot decide what to take off your plate, you simply let them sit there. Then a lot of times a little olive rolls off the plate. Let them be on the plate and shove this off to the side so you can eat what you want. Don't allow yourself to get involved so energetically that you're worrying. Simply allow it to be there. Call it an option. Call it a side dish.

When we talked before about abundance, we said that in order to shift the way that you felt about credit card bills and things that were due, was for you to feel gratitude for this bill coming in because the money allowed you to do whatever you needed to do at that time. You always have a choice and sometimes the choice is how you react to it, how much energy you give it, how you feel about it, and that shifts everything. There's always a choice in every matter. Choice does matter.

In terms of business, I have many choices and am not sure which way to turn.

Understand that there are no new ideas. Everything that is out there is out there. It just happens to be who taps into that information and pull it into physicality. If you didn't pull it into physicality, someone else would tune into the radio dial and get that information. Right now you need to choose which you'd like to see to fruition, those you'd like to share with others, or others that are great ideas that you'll let go so someone else can tune into them and get them. When you decide which is most important to you, put your energy into that and do what you need to do. Absolutely trust your guidance and your guidance alone.

Standing for Who You Are

How do I be who I am and not someone that others find acceptable?

It's a very valid concern. It's something that is touching the lives of each person in this room and the fact that there is not one person in this room who can continue to hide and not stand firmly for your convictions whether they be about your personal life, your spiritual beliefs, political views, whatever it is, this is the year for each and every one of you to stand up and say, "This is who I am and this is what I believe."

There are a couple of things you can do. We truly recommend you be who you are and believe what you believe and do not let anyone discount you. You do not have to take abuse. When you speak about who you are and what you believe in, it's just a matter of sharing, it's not a personal attack on anyone. It's simply sharing what you believe in. If you put that energy into it, it will shift the energy in the room.

The second thing is, and this is more difficult for all of you, when you are with people who have different beliefs than you, do not take it personally. You must understand they are doing the best they can with who they are. They are perfect in their own life right at that moment. That is all there is and all there can be.

Number one, realize that you can change no person. Number two, don't try and change their political beliefs. Allow yourself to be firm and stay grounded in who you are. Do not allow them to knock you over with their words. Before a gathering, breathe in the grounded energy. Pull it up from your feet and breathe down your spirit. Continue to create the complete circle of grounded energy flowing up to spirit and back down again. You must stay connected that way at all times.

Remember the breath and allow yourself to be able to be flexible, but not blown over. If you're strong in your energy, nothing can harm you. Get very rooted in who you are. Nothing will faze you after that.

We must walk our walk and talk our talk every moment of every day. You must remember who you are. To do that is to remember the soul that you are. To do that is to remember you are in the human body; that you are integrated, a spiritual human being. When you are integrated, nothing can stop you. No one can harm you. No wolves can get you.

There are no shoulds. It simply is.

A Beginning

So as you move into your being, we just want to remind all of you that this is the year to focus on your life, your happiness. It is time to take a look at your plate and say, "What is the food I like and what is it I don't want to eat any longer?" It is imperative that every breath you take, every thought you have, every move you make, be of focus and total clarity. That you live your life to the fullest, that you be in joy, that you are willing to risk, to try new things because if they don't work out, you hop to the next boat.

It's not about failure. It's about taking the chance and having choices. You are all very connected to each other and the non-physicals and us, *The Band*. Our connections will continue on whether we're in the same room at the same time or not. Open up to your guidance and listen, taking care of yourselves first. Putting the gas in your own tank and making sure the tires are in good condition too.

Part of your path and connection is really to be of service and bring back that spiritual knowledge into your peer groups and those that you serve. The more that you are able to touch other people's lives in many different aspects, the more on your path you are. It is not about focusing, and we say this to all of you, it is not about focusing narrowly in your life anymore. It is about opening up and experiencing all. Your life is about expanding what you do; to not just serve the individual, but to serve a larger population of individuals through your teaching.

Shift the way you experience the guidance of your angels, your personal guides, *The Band*. You are teachers as well. You are our guides. You are telling us this is the area of life where people are experiencing difficulty or challenges. We say, "How can we in the nonphysical make that experience more joyful, more informative and more helpful?"

We wish to say to each and every one of you is open your arms. Embrace life. Find every moment joyful. Allow it to teach you and grow and participate in being a spiritual human being. If you go about your daily life with worry, concern, drudgery, or fear, then you are not living your life to the fullest. Embrace your life now! Though you may have physical things, though you may have mental things, financial things that are ever-present, know this is part of the experience of life. You are not in it alone. You never have been alone, and you never will be.

Everywhere you go, you have *The Band* with you. You have us in the nonphysical, and we have you in the physical. It is very mutual. We are learning from your lives, from your experiences. It is not that we on the nonphysical side know it all. We do not. It is simply that we are able to tap into information more easily. It is a circle.

What you teach us we are able to experience and therefore we are able to give you back information that you are able to experience. This is not a one-way street of information coming out.

We thank you so much for being here and we look forward to our continued journey with you.

Namaste

About the Author

Willow Sibert is a third-generation psychic and channel as well as a successful businesswoman who works with a group energy called '*The Band*.' Together they provide clarity and guidance that can help you move forward in your own life. Often with humor and always with love, universal knowledge is communicated through Willow's down-to-earth practicality and professionalism. An unbeatable combination!

Willow lives in southern Arizona amidst beautiful mountain ranges (and cacti). She has experienced psychic phenomena since childhood. Her mother was one of a long line of psychics on the women's side, and her father's family attended a Spiritualist church. Willow began sensing a nearby nonphysical entity during her meditations in the late 1990's, and she began channeling *The Band* for friends and family soon after that.

Meanwhile, she has lived a many-faceted life, from her early days as a wife and step-mother to a corporate trainer to a practicing certified consulting hypnotist, with specialized training in both conventional hypnosis for habit change and past life regression hypnosis. Two little rescue dogs keep her well-grounded and humble. When the dogs allow it, she enjoys going for long walks, gardening, and reading.

Claim Your Free Gift

Dear Reader,

Thank you so much for reading this book! The Band and I are most appreciative of your interest in the information we share.

In further appreciation, please claim your free gift to experience a video of one of our previously-recorded channeled sessions as they happened in the early days, when Willow and *The Band* first began speaking to the public.

Visit this link to register and watch the full session – https://www.channelingwithwillow.com/free-channeled-session

Review This Book

Review this book on the Bookseller site where you got it originally...

Just visit the book page for and scroll down below the *About the Author* section on the book page.

Once there, you can click the "**Review this product**" link in the left-hand column, just below existing Customer reviews.

If you run into any issues posting an Amazon review, try posting one on GoodReads.com or BookBub.com

Please share an honest review *(and, if you received an Advance Reader Copy (ARC) Team copy of the book, please say so in your review).*

Made in the USA
Coppell, TX
23 November 2024